O Yes We Breathe

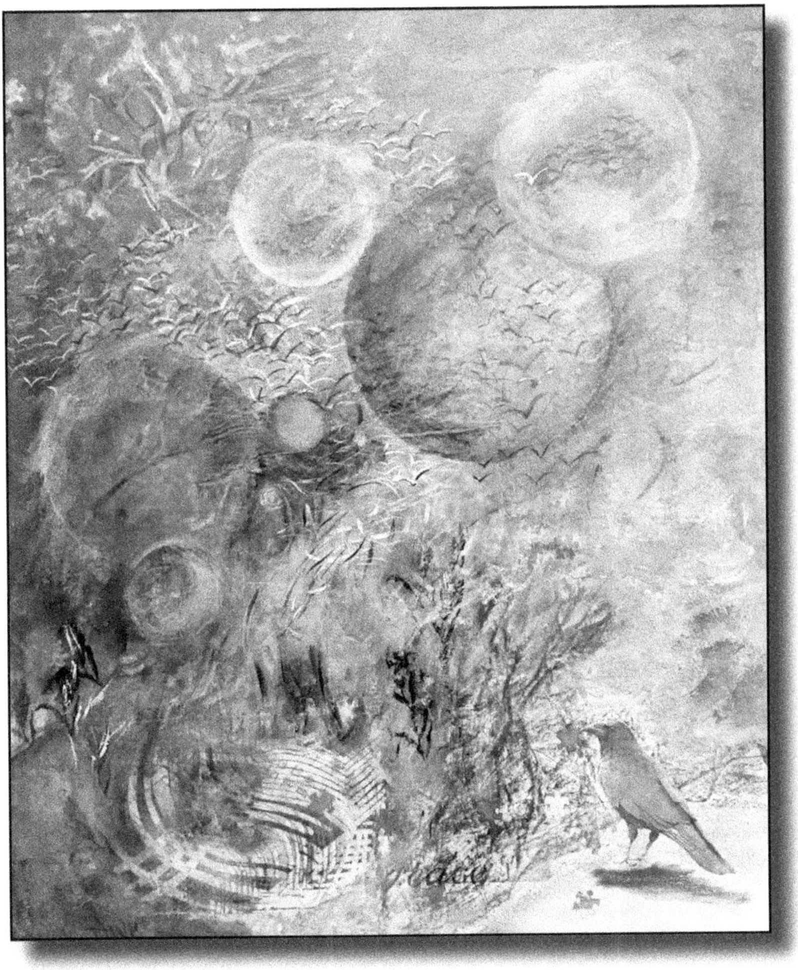

Gary Thomas

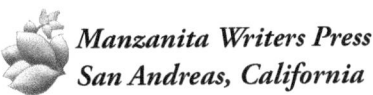
Manzanita Writers Press
San Andreas, California

O Yes We Breathe
Copyright © 2024 by Gary Thomas

All rights reserved. No part of this book may be used, stored in a retrieval system, reproduced in any manner, electronic, mechanical, photocopy, recording, or using other media without written permission from the author or publisher.

ISBN: 978-1-952314-13-1
Library of Congress Control Number: 2024923519

Published by:
    Manzanita Writers Press
    San Andreas, CA
    manzapress.com
    manzanitawp@gmail.com

Cover Photograph: Piecing It Back Together by Ann Williams-Bailey
Author Bio Photo: Jack Sutton
Book & Cover Design: Joyce Dedini-Runnells

For information contact author:
    Gary Thomas
    rasselas9@charter.net
    garyet99@gmail.com

Stagger onward rejoicing . . .

——*W. H. Auden, "Atlantis"*

——For All Those Who Have, Do, and Will——

Table of Contents

Prologue: A Firestarter — 7

Hard News & Kittens in Trees

Almost Too Early, The Anchorman Said, — 11
Chester Drawers — 12
Children's Crusade — 13
How We Look Today (January 2017) — 14
Hurricane Weeps — 16
Stars and Garters, Once Upon — 18
Mythology: An Update — 20
April 9th ——This Day in Mystery — 21
Today, — 22

If Memory Serves

Crossbred — 24
There's This — 26
City Hospital, Modesto, California,
    October 22, 1948 — 27
Christmas Morning in My Roy Rogers Bathrobe — 28
Sunday Drivers, the Fifties — 30
We All Scream — 31
Gullywasher — 32
Heat Wave — 34
I Remember Days When I Never Thought Twice
    About What Was Farther Off — 35
Sandstone Fireplace — 36
To the Grindstone — 38
Reading *The Horrors of Blood Hollow* — 40
Denny — 42
Overcooked Okra at the Vista 6 — 44
Pitchforking the Cat, or What Remains — 46
The Only Things—— — 48
The Reasons I Became — 50
    a One-Room Shack This Month — 50
Liaisons Ordinaires — 51

Apathy Breaks Up with Me

I Wish You Were You — 53
Lunacized — 54
So — 55

Table of Contents

Breathing Rooms	56
Insectaria	58
Sonnet Catch XXII from the Papuese	59
When You I	60
Widow's Weeds	62
You Are Right, Of Course	63
Your Fellow Traveler	64
Try This	65
Valentines	66

Ready to Step Into Waves

Brood	68
Renascence	69
Annus Mirabilis	70
Seated by a Window in Southwest Seattle	72
Intravenous	73
Letting Go Gladly	74
This Afternoon	75
Hugely Beautiful	76
My Best Impersonation of a Harbor Seal	77
Rationalism	78
The Nut Grass Groove	79
Epistolary	80
In Which I Imagine Writing at a Standing Desk	81
Mense Octobri Gratiae	82
Upper Falls, Lower Falls, Valley Floor	84
Low Arcanum	85
Some Prayers on a Monday	86
Towards the Splendid City	88
(Nobel Lecture, December 13, 1971)	88
The Eyebrows On It	90
Uncertainty	91
Zehn Gebehtsachen (Ten Prayer Things)	92
A Respiration	95
Epilogue: Widdershins	96
Gratitudes	97
Acknowledgements	98
About the Author	99

Prologue: A Firestarter

Shivering in early morning
                next to the old stove,

you build a fire out of juniper
                and yesterday's news.

The aroma of sparks assures you
                there is a future for you.

Your backbone slips into place.
                So do your eyes, which just now

fix on some snowbirds
                escaped from your soul's sockets.

You stretch your handful of seeds to them,
                and they come to feed. The stove starts

tapping its code of heat and hope,
                its need for another log. You catch.

Hard News & Kittens in Trees

Almost Too Early, The Anchorman Said,

to be talking about any repercussions
of the air strikes, the surface-to-air missiles,
the ground war just beginning.

This just in——
                the thunderstorm,
                the shoot-out in the city
                      so close.

After this message,
coming up——
                the latest deportations
                    of children,
            a kitten stuck in a tree
                    with an escaped python,
            politicians who might
                    throw their hats,
            celebrities who might have
                    baby bumps,
            which cellphone apps
                    are trending,

and if there's time,
                the names of the dead,
                which ones can be blamed most
                    for their own bad timing,
            and
            how the kitten rescued
                the big snake
                      almost too late.

Chester Drawers

I was fifteen, a sophomore, before
I learned from a new friend's laughter
there were no such things as chester drawers.
My Midwestern mother commanded I put away
everything she squashed and starched
on the shiny steel mangle——
sheets, pants, shirts, even socks ——
in my room, her room, any room
with a chest-of-drawers,
compartments small, lean,
right-angled enough to hold
hot creased fabric harvested
from steam and pressure.

Yes, Ma'am——I stacked my Levi's and T's
crisp as a corporal's khakis, lowered them
into dresser drawers like cotton corpses.
unaware as an ingénue that other sophomores
whose mothers never used a mangle
would find themselves too soon in holes,
bags, shelves, drawers, their names displayed
in the creases of a shiny black wall.

Children's Crusade

We know now that what we were told had happened in 1212 was a myth and there was no deluge of children who believed seas would part so they could saunter to a remote Holy Land where they would be welcomed like kin but instead were sold into slavery or died along the way then vanished or ascended

Now they cross our river and we're afraid which is the actual problem not that they are children utterly alone escaping something worse than the journey and we're anxious they might breathe too much of our pilgrim-proud air eat too much of our food their cousins to the north stooped and harvested to shoulder us out of a land we waged war upon to keep to ourselves so we are afraid of children who might get too close who might stay next door who might grow up safe

How We Look Today (January 2017)

*Do all the good you can, by all the means you can,
in all the ways you can, in all the places you can,
at all the times you can, to all the people you can,
as long as ever you can.*
———*attributed to John Wesley*

Water   River   Spirit   Grace———

Hard to remember blessings when
our screens and speakers spit hatred
masked as greatness
                        when
our friends and our strangers have slipped
in the swelter of blood we could not staunch———

So hard that we must *resolve* to be patient,
decide to tell ourselves out loud———

> *Remember to breathe
> even when the lies damn near choke us out
> even as the apathy around us rises like fog
> on a swamp.*
>
> *Stand with those who share the common flame,
> withstand those who would steal it.*
>
> *Look*———*not at a gallery of carnival mirrors,
> but through all the day's open windows.*
>
> *Find our own steady hands at the ends of our arms
> and use them each moment to uphold those that tremble.*
>
> *Make ready to serve. Serve. Clean up after.*

*Listen deep, look deeper into, through,
beyond what's constituted, then*

Learn deepest——how to move

like water,

like a river,

like spirit,

like grace:

                not at, but through.

Hurricane Weeps

You can dance in a hurricane
But only if you're standing in the eye
——Brandi Carlile, "The Eye"

Hurricane weeps for us mortals
as it dismembers our dwellings,
landscape, habits, diaries.
Should we weep for it as it withers
suddenly, becomes mere wind,
rests, builds strength to become
Cyclone in another hemisphere?
Can it help itself? Could *we*
help ourselves as we pour the drink
that will mash the accelerator?
Do we help any mortals in the path
of what will shatter them?
We sleep with one eye open,
hide as if shelter were our one future.

Ford F-150 storms from the tears of the spouse,
spits broken glass and orange dirt in a pillar
from tires familiar with this fury. Terminus
uncertain as sky. Blood alcohol level predictable
as counterclockwise apology followed by slow
dancing inside the eyewall of their marriage.
Any questions anyone requires remain sealed
in their imploding condo.
Blackhawk gyres and sweeps for victims.
Widdershins blades named
Search, Rescue, Retrieve, Survive
chuff and churn as Blackhawk scans
surviving roofs, soaked bodies shivering
on any highest ground or structure,
wide eyes pleading for grace wherever
it materializes, however human light
dances through wreckage to help new kin,
carry them to some unknown safety
fragile as any fugitive ambience.
How are any of us still alive?

Stars and Garters, Once Upon

Those of you in the 31st Century——
or 22nd if we don't make sense of this one——
might like to know what we used to say
when we were astonished or wanted to tell
a story about when we gasped.
                  Strike that.
                                        Hello, humans,
if you have no hope of centuries ahead, or
just *about* remember what a century was once.
Upon all the stars that are left, I swear we
were still working with some astonishment
at sussing out why ice melted and winters
brought us toads and boils.

When we went to zoos and museums when
there were zoos and museums, we gasped
at macaws, gaped at Rothko's scarlets and
blacks, felt smug we could draw analogies
and a big dipper on a beer mat.

We said *Crazy* a lot whether we adored
or despised someone, something——
a verdict, a Mars mission, anything
we might have to spend time imagining,
determining, making amends over.

We watched televised competitions in fashion,
haute cuisine, cupcakes, candy sculpture, pottery,
swordcraft, prosthetic makeup, tattoos, and,
well, *anything* because it was on.
We knew the names of contestants
and which season they lost
or which piece of dreck made them stars.
If there had been a post-wedding challenge
to sew and launch the bluest garter,
we'd have saved the date for its premiere.

Some of us got Ph.Ds for research on *embolalia*
(or *embololalia*) and could sing arias of *uh*s,
*um*s, *like*s, and *yaknow*s with a *noproblem* coda.
A few of us dropped *Ewww* and *Cute*
into any book club or bar crawl discourse
to nods and chuckles, and everyone knew
that *viral* or *zoom* were last year's buzz.
We were so *adept*, so *absorbed*, so *incognizant*.

If there's still history when you are, you know
something of us, that love was here
along with knees on necks,
that flop sweat thudded
and a still small voice prodded,
that we half-tried
to do something better
than what we knew——
just that, as Hirshfield wrote,
we did not-enough.

Could be you're the happy ending. Maybe
you'll be the ones to amaze the universe,
make it drop its cosmic jaw and chuckle
at its own irony. O my stars.

Mythology: An Update

When did it come to be about daggers,
shape thermostat spats into cul-de-sacs,
worst restaurant in town endured again
and again, face-to-face a yard apart,
their paltry assurances on repeat?

A marriage sound enough for the season
from which it sprang now gasps for evergreen
ghosts of embraces that healed. Duration
squeezed this pair into grim pomegranates
of need, pulpy garnet blisters sundered
from shared membranes of lies and animus.

So many means to split the climaxed fruit
of Persephone, to cleave sharply all
that was joined, or to cleave to what may yet
be sweet as narcissi in lavish spring.

April 9th ——This Day in Mystery

Phil Ochs hanged himself in Far Rockaway
as I sat in a statistics class in Turlock
      a Friday 47 years ago the radio played Ochs'
        The War is Over

Soviet troops used entrenching tools
to kill Georgians as my school district
imposed new standardized tests
      a Friday 34 years ago CDs still spun Madonna's
        Like a Prayer

Massacre in Palestine   riots in Bogotá
      maneuvers in post-Brit Burma
as not-yet-I squirmed fussed waited to enter
the postwar atmosphere
      a Friday 75 years ago 78's sang Peggy Lee's
        Mañana (Is Soon Enough for Me)

I bought an LP because Lester Bangs said
it was the future of rock and roll
I bought another LP because
the shrink-wrap sticker said
it was the only band that mattered
        and this was true at the time
        as music is always true
        but this time
        the cruelest month lasts too long
        memory and desire would like a divorce
        the dead won't stay buried
        but busy themselves
        being born on repeat

Tomorrow no matter what month——
always mystery——
Eliot's dull roots and spring rain mix-taped
with the day we survive to see——
a reminder of the ones worth sunlight.

Today,

what I have been is not historic
or unpunctuated by loss,
undone by unwisdom.
I who am ever getting myself lost
in and for the moment
wear my faded turquoise
Citizen of Quotidiana
t-shirt not as uniform, but
as a raiment of aspiration.

Today does not know where
it is going, other than tonight.
Today's unscripted program
is already in progress.
On the path, off the trail
is one Way, Gary Snyder wrote,
so I continue.

Pausing is part of it. *Yet* is another.
Seven decades and change
is only one teacher.
A dove's egg as it rends open
is one beginning of wisdom.

Tomorrow will worry about
itself, I've been told, and I wish
I could unworry more.
Right now I'm watching
this egg reveal what it has
pending. Imminence ain't
answers, but in between
ain't all that awful, either.
Is that a beak? If so, what
will be wings will follow.
So will I. Today, thanks.

after Lucille Clifton's "i am not done yet"

If Memory Serves

Crossbred

I come from a long line of line-crossers——
        poor mutts who left,
        looked for anyplace
        less harsh than the land
        that abandoned them
        to fend, starve, move out

So——
        hardtack passage over
        two and a half meridians
        to strange sod, quare sheep,
        odd slate rubble and soft coal
        glossy as new iridescent sin

farmers, miners,	
	Taffy, Geordie, Gog
once-in-a-while grocers	
	store-lubber choirboys
husbands who waited	
	widowers pending
for wives and plentyn	
	dependents pending
till they could afford	
	commoners' marriage
a next escape west	
	a Welsh skedaddle

So——

    mule wagons,   piles of shit,
    stolen horses,   piles of shit,
    freight trains,   piles of soft coal,
    departure,   dust,   destination

Then an outcasts' town called Two Timbers,
    or Two Sticks if after the Crash———
        a family with seed potatoes
        wrapped in wet burlap roped inside
        bumpers of a Model A Ford
        crosses seven state lines to plant beans,
        milk Holsteins,
            fend   *hardscrabble*
        shift.   *budge along*
            replant.   *just like Okies*
                remarry   *a dragged-out widower*

I come from constellations
of Old Country Southern Midwest nomads———
a long line of migrant names unstoried even to me
who pointed at lines they thought they saw in the sky
and traced them into soil too often not theirs———
so now I miss who they might have been proud to be———
crossbred and here for a spell.

There's This

      There's this honeymoon portrait
of my father and mother   really just
a Brownie snap taken by an invisible stranger.
      Selfies were not a thing in '37.

      They're happy and free of the work
they've left for this sparkling trip to Yosemite,
the work they'll need to do when they begin
their everyday lives together——and I
won't exist for nearly a dozen years.

      I never saw this alluring pose of hers
or his fresh ardor and amazement at his luck.
For me, they were only *them*——my very own
world-openers who made me do the good things,
made fresh-disced soil a farmer boy's playground.

      On their off-white bedroom wall
in its plain black frame still perched staunchly
on the shaky shadowy nightstand of my memory
is the shimmer of my dead parents happy in 1937,
the grasp that I am here now because of that——
so there's this.

City Hospital, Modesto, California, October 22, 1948

In that time, the custom for ladies of a certain age
was to imitate the *materfamilias* of MacDuff
or Julius Caesar and arrange for their only-born
to be untimely ripped into this world, even though
Harry Truman was still its chief executive.

My mother made an appointment for my birth,
did not want it to be inconvenient for me
in later years to have to share her birthday
(my original due date) and scheduled my arrival
two days early. So, out of maternal courtesy,

here I was, a round-headed wonder,
eager to be punctual ever after
since I had already
predated myself.

Christmas Morning in My Roy Rogers Bathrobe

I suspend an argyle sock half-filled with an orange
and some Brazil nuts in one hand,
a box of Roy Rogers Classy brand spurs in the other.
The bulk of my other presents draped over
a dining room chair have the same theme:
King of the Cowboys
double-cap-pistol & holster set,
waxed black boots,
matching vest & chaps
with a branding iron hieroglyphics motif.

Here is Joy itself
and an overwhelm of what will be
once the debris has been doublechecked
for anything left over,
when I can go outside
to be Roy and an outlaw
simultaneously,
aroma of oak blaze
from the fireplace my father made
blent with unbaled alfalfa in troughs
and phosphorus from scarlet roll caps
ignited in the greystone Yule air.

I am king cowboy of this meager ranch where
my family wrangles peaches and dairy cows.
My hands never tire of squeezing the triggers
of both dark pistols, listening for the cheap metal
clicks and *cracks* just after, shameless, guileless,
unaware of what this will mean later when
bittersweet blood sprouts in my mouth

from gnawing my cheek in fear, when
sour howls ascend from other throats as they
grieve for me when one, then both parents
are gone and what remains is this black-and-white
reminder of one over-gifted Christmas morning,
a fantasy built from parents' naïve benevolence
and a child's gullible faith in happy trails sung
by a blithe screen cowboy named Leonard Sly.
Click.

Sunday Drivers, the Fifties

After church we drove home for pot roast.
Then my father decided where we would point

our two-tone grey Dodge Coronet with Hydramatic
transmission, choosing the back roads he knew

my mother would love, where were wildflowers,
even in early March, someone's potted geraniums

to admire. *Just an hour or two, Honey——*
then I'll need to get a few acres disked before dark.

She would smile, knowing how much he liked to stop
for a fruit stand bargain, how little he really wanted

to climb on the tractor on a Sunday. The radio was
tuned to KTRB——Rose Maddox and her Brothers

sometimes played live those afternoons, silly giggles
accompanying our cruise through the valley we used

to make a living the other six days, before this day
breathed its languid air through four open windows

at forty-five miles an hour. Or two.

We All Scream

The day the ice cream truck played
Guns and Roses instead of Stephen Foster
or Turkey in the Straw,
all the push-ups and popsicles melted
into day-glo puddles

and chaos wore a waffle-cone crown.
Even cats slipped in snow-cone syrup.

It wasn't even hot enough
to unplug kids from X-boxes and Playstations
and scoop them into the street in search
of plain vanilla, eager chocolate,
desperate strawberry——

——just an early summer jungle
welcoming anyone who would open a door
to scamper after butterfat in its most perfect form,
original sinlessness unshattered
by guns, roses, or any growing up at all.

Gullywasher

I heard it anytime the rivers rose, the levees broke,
our orchard contorted itself into
Bunyan's Slough of Despond——

Yehhp, thattuz a real gullywasher. Any 4-in-the-morning
from Election Day to April Fools, I could figure
to be stirred from my flannel sheets to see
my father's face tell me
    Grab a shovel,
follow him to the fields,
    dig fast and strong
as I could.
    Shore up, shore up, follow the lead edge
    of your last shovelful,
and I would because it mattered to him
and was mattering to me,
till the levee held fast against the surge
and I'd slog back to bed
or brace my back against our rural route mailbox,
wait for the diesel bluster of our school bus
as it wallowed through puddles and road ponds
left by the drench.

I'd watch it plow the length of our road,
cowcatch cataracts of froth and sludge
into our neighbors' fields.
When it slowed enough for its waves to ebb
into ripples, I'd board, expecting to be bored
by recess, the flood of noise and baloney at lunch,
the absurdities of New Math.

Some crumbs of luster——
a poem in our basal readers,
a song from the state-approved *American Singer*
against the gullywash of grade school ennui.
Capote called it *a sky that stops*, that sensible horizon
of others' fear of more-than-this.
This morning my qualms of what-comes-next
have receded, cleared enough to become mysteries.
Forecasts augur *cold and dry*, skies are boundless as
I listen deep for that farmer's voice——
    Shore up, shore up . . .

Heat Wave

Three in the morning. Still hot enough to melt breath.
Throat like steak under sandpaper.
Even with the overhead fan,
heat waves its nettle brush over my belly,
under my arms, in between each leg hair.

I hear the vehemence of eight days' incessant swelter——
so much like the brick incinerator
at my grade school when I was eight,
and the janitor let me feed it with milk cartons
from Friday's fish-stick lunch. Their wax hissed
along with the scalded sour milk still left,
smoke oozing through the cracks in the masonry.

I learned how to close those sheet-iron doors
with his broomstick, and the black roar
of what burned rose into a small-town sky,
like the crematoria I would read about later.
I wondered then if books were lit to burn bodies,
since they'd been used to build rallies before,
hate shimmering from pages,
faces and arms angled upward,
uniform as fireplaced paragraphs.

The bedroom walls and roof still tick, contract,
grumble from the fever this closed-in August brings.
I navigate these dark swells, become spectator,
reflector, smoke. The temperature drops.
I draw a full breath for the first time in hours.
I could almost eat something, wash it down
with something cold, soft, benign. Four o'clock.

I Remember Days When I Never Thought Twice About What Was Farther Off

after a line in "How We Were Transfigured"
—— *Eavan Boland*

I was making something from mud. Pleased no one was near in case I failed. Sure my dad's tractor was doing its work somewhere I couldn't see as it coughed and warbled through the orchard.

Days that lasted till dinnertime or as soon as I finished that last chore by flashlight. No ambition other than to watch *Maverick* undisturbed. Homework done enough. Oreos within reach.

News was Huntley, Brinkley, and how McCovey, Cepeda, and Mays did that day. Church was 5 times a week without question, especially hymns, even when my dad stopped being.

And then, I want to say, as if what followed from farther off was a snap of fingers. Instead, and not of a sudden, Tet was
a part of my vocabulary, as were Tonkin Bay, Birmingham, Berlin, Beatles, Dallas, Dylan, and Dream.

And I never thought just once again.

Sandstone Fireplace

My father is using the small chisel now,
tapping lightly on the edges
of each sandstone slab,
moving from stone to stone,
chips of pale yellow and soft red
littering the lawn like spilled birdseed.

He has quarried and carried each piece
from the cliffs above the riverbanks,
sweated and grunted them each
onto the Ford flatbed, roped them
around the tie-downs tightly,
cinched them securely
with the deft knots he is famous for,
edged the truck on its weight-squashed tires
the twenty-five miles to our farm,
where he unloads each one carefully
onto the backyard under the locust trees
dropping their own fluttering burden
on the same lawn as the stones.

He mixes the mortar with his mason's certainty,
trowels each stone only apparently at random,
steps back each time after slapping each stone
into its new home and place in the world,
until the facade of the fireplace
is fixed and firm as each part of each tier,
until the ceiling is reached,
until he steps back and announces,
"She's done, I figure,"
and goes to wash up.

I want to start a fire right away
to see how it will draw——
he has taught me what "draw" means——
but he says,
"It has to cure some yet."
I do not know what "cure" has to do
with a fireplace, or stone, for that matter,
but I do not doubt him.
He has built it——he must know
how long things take, even if it means waiting
as long as it took the sandstone to make itself.

To the Grindstone

My father calls it a treadlestone.
I am not strong enough for it,
not strong enough to help it
do its work, not strong
or tall enough yet
even to press the foot treadles
with enough authority
to start the grave grey wheel spinning
or sit in the steel saddle while trying.

In the dusty farmhouse workroom,
my father helps me find
the rhythm of the stone——
    Just getting you started——
gives it a soft nudge forward at the top,
as he had when he taught me to ride
the same rusty red bicycle
my five older brothers pedaled
into their futures.

    I'd watched him sharpen axes and hoes,
    but the first blade he gave me to hone
    was his own——the jackknife he used
    to whittle pruned peach branches
    into numbers for our farmhouse,
    the blade he'd carved red-yellow clings
    into ripe slices of summer,
    the perfect fuel for boys
    who need to grow strong enough
    to use stone tools, tall enough
    to stand up when the work is done
    and see the glint of what needs to be
    sharp enough to do its work well.

Now with a firmer shove, he sits and pedals
till it spins and rumbles, ready for me
to press a blade edge against its rolling bulk
and purpose as I carefully find the whisper
a knife can make as its bevel is made just right.
My father nods and I imagine we have made
even this grindstone proud
to lose a little of itself
to something so keen.

Reading *The Horrors of Blood Hollow*

I was ten, waiting to be scared
at least as much as I was relieved
that this book wasn't scaring me at all——
at least not any more than I'd been already
by a black-and-white B feature whose name
I no longer recall——double-billed with *The Fly*.

All I really remember is a fleshlike fungus
called *blood rust* infecting all actors,
killing them hideously, noisily, satisfactorily.
I wasn't sure then or now
why or how this was accomplished,
but was sufficiently creeped out
by the connection between slime on the screen
and sneakers sticking to the theatre floor
to ignore the blood rust's motivation or strategy.

Of course, I may have this all mixed up with *The Blob*,
which didn't scare me, but certainly made me avoid
raspberry jam for a full year
after seeing all the flesh-eating annihilation
wrought by this amorphous Technicolor compote.

The people in the *Blood Hollow* book get killed
by some mountain-folk menace who cuts them up,
puts them up as pickled preserves
resembling *patas de puerco*
on a grander scale,
brimful of brine and blood sugar,
overripe and rusty as anything
packaged in Hollywood.

Seventy-odd years later, I am thinking
of the Airport Drive-in in Santa Barbara,
where one late summer early '70's night
I binged on a triple-bill horror-and-gore fest.
Only one of the three films scared me——
sandpapery black-and-white footage, still garish,
made-outside-Pittsburgh in a cemetery
with Johnny and Barbara, brother and sister
who chuckle, bored with their family duties
and floral tributes, then are attacked without warning
by a middle-aged drudge in a black raincoat
who looks like his head has been doused with Clorox.

By the second reel, as Barbara
climbs to the top of a curving staircase
of an unfamiliar farmhouse,
discovers at the very top
a semi-devoured skull,
I was already backing out of the drive-in,
spitting gravel, ignoring
the honked complaints and catcalls
of the jaded clientele
whose flesh did not fester and crawl
as mine did at the original *Night of the Living Dead.*

I also think of horrors that have happened since
to scare me more than those naive films:
real skulls devoured by bullets,
a plague more virulent
than the Hollywood Strain,

daily/nightly invasions on the living
by the disciples of death,
the hollow hopes and promises
offered by so many hollow men,
the vacancy and vanity of narrowed lives.
I find no blood hollow anymore.

Denny

First we were friends because we were picked on——
the odd ones not picked for games till last.
We grew to be easy with each other's failure,
glad to lose out if it meant we could win
some time for our own small sports——mumbley-peg,
monkey bars, tetherball, those homemade kites
flung into March gales, dared in October gusts.
We were farm boys, used to working peaches,
almonds, our tractors and hand tools ground down
by bigger hands, whittled down to fit ours
so we could become what our fathers were.

We never did. We stayed friends till high school
called us to what we never imagined:
a grey domain of strangers divided
by diversions, classes, capacities.
We stopped calling or greeting each other
in the hallways. Even on the same bus,
we rambled homeward by different roads.
Breath upon breath, we forgot each other.

Many million respirations later,
my wife and I needed a new car——
which is to say a hulk of a van
for the dull tools, bright toys
a family amasses in between
its mutual destinations.
I called the biggest dealership
to get the best deal. You answered.
We were each of us surprised.
We reminisced, reminded each other

how long it had been. We caught up,
bargained. Because we were no longer
familiar, we found it easy to agree
we could not work out a deal,
our split perspectives dividing us again.
We were both glad to end the conversation,
and since then have managed
to lose each other's numbers
and reasons to keep them.
Like mumbley-peg, sometimes
an accustomed blade
breaks badly,
or we choose different kites,
other winds.

Overcooked Okra at the Vista 6

It was Oregon.
It was July.
You were there,
a cut-rate counterfeit
of the blandest imitation
of hospitality in the nation,
and we were bone-tired enough
to accept your accommodations:
icy showerhead spurting
in climactic thuds,
coin-play black&white TV
going silent and cold
as your Magic Fingers
just before *Ben-Hur*'s chariot race.
Our bed's mattress fit us like a bowl
molded over the decades
by the bodies
of your previous
unwary guest victims.
Your complimentary brunch
consisted of mortadella
and bologna sliced
so long ago
they both curled
at their edges,
smacking of what
we'd slept on——
or in, depending
on your taste
in prepositions applicable
to slumber furniture.

But I digress——
your singular most
sinister buffet item
was the Okra Surprise——
the surprise being it was there at all,
bearing a resemblance to
and consistency of
chartreuse mincemeat
and fresh mucilage.
To be honest,
I've never liked
okra much, slime
being so integral
to its essence,
but what would gumbo be
without it?
As long as it's green
and not animal protein,
I'll bite, but what *really* bit
was *your* kind of green:
the same as
the pea-tinted
crusty loo-mold
in every corner
of every room.

Even now, long after our stay
that excruciating night
of mutual cringing,
we still shudder whenever
we hear these three words,
whatever the context:
Vista. Six. Okra.

Pitchforking the Cat, or What Remains

For days, a keen pungency broadcasts her quietus.
Acrid as she is, I who lack her natural aptitude
cannot sniff out her singular body in my backyard,
where honeysuckle joins sharp battle with lantana.

At last I breathe fully what she now exhales forever.
Under an old azalea crowded by volunteers
from an unremembered rosebush, I see her,
motionless against the periwinkles, as if she were
running sideways in midnight green.

Unowned by anyone ever, we said, *some neighbor's
mongrel or a stray entirely*, she splays her fangs at death.
White worms that will be flies tunnel toward her core,
that dynamo now an erstwhile engine of purrs and yawps.

I locate a sturdy shovel and splintered pitchfork,
its tines rusting from the last time I slung
moldering camphor leaves into the compost bin,
retrieve the dented trash can, find a new 4 mil trash bag,
fit it into the can's rigid maw, search for a patch
of unspaded soil, start the solemn excavation.

I don't know what I am doing until I am doing it.
I draw in my breath and gorge, slip four slender prongs
under her sad mass. I do not pet her, even with gloves,
though my hands know they should. Gently as I know,
I lift what is left of her into the black plastic void,
and with silent prayers for her grimalkin soul, dig deeper,
lower the bag beneath a horizon too well known.
I cover her up, spare myself nothing about my part
in this, accept that this creature I never met is gone.

Another use for a pitchfork,
more charcoal fur to moulder,
new intimations of all impermanence.
A strange hollow dent in the earth.
Another name only she knows.

The Only Things——

What my mother used every day,
what my father used till it couldn't be,
what I still have and use that was theirs——

yellow / green / red / blue Pyrex bowls
        nesting inside each other until
                filled with flour, sugar, other wonders:

hickory-handled lopping shears for
hedges, peach tree limbs at pruning time,
broken or burst hoses needing repair,
anything needing finality or a fresh start.

ivory ceramic salt & pepper shakers bigger
than a clenched fist, meant for biding handily
on a stovetop, used there, then brought
to the kitchen table to season eggs, fried chicken,
sliced spuds still bubbling after bobbing on the surface
of bacon grease in a cast iron skillet bigger
than any farmer's stomach.

serrated sling blade, double-edged axe, hatchet
with keen bits that sparkled as they cleared bull nettles,
dead trees, busted boxes from a landscape I still see
with my thousand-yard stare built of seven-plus decades
of being a farmer's son with no farm.

sandstone block on a front porch——what remains
        of a fireplace my father built,
           where he taught me fire-craft
           and a way to use fear as fuel.

the skillet where my mother taught me how
        chicken should be fried,
and the one I ruined,
                left on the burner too long
                        till black smoke swarmed
                  this newer kitchen,
          plunged into a cold soapy sink,
          turned into a bottom warped
                and awkward as a cheap wok
                mocking me justly for my neglect.

So I list what was used, used up,
still used, like this thing telling you
about the only things left of them
other than their common energies
radiating as I write the only thing
I know how.

The Reasons I Became
a One-Room Shack This Month

April 2020

At first it was *easy*: eat, read, watch, listen, write, sleep,
repeat in any order or not. *Rustic* in that my wife tried
to bake bread from a levain and we attempted to eat
the whole wheat discus that thudded from the oven.
Ah, and it's been downright *cozy* feeling my four
walls, one carpet and ceiling as they hug me closer
by the hour. Tonight, I snuck outside to catch the
pink-moon perigee-syzygy, begged it to hug me, kiss
me with its full-on lunacy, but just missed the best
part of the ellipse. Sparrows, finches, and jays are
just outside to be my flash mobs, mobilized by my
broadcast of seeds and meal worms. You've read
this far and wonder about the whys. They're the
same *becauses* as yours: I'm old and infirm enough
to catch IT, and God gave me just enough brains
to seek the shelter I've become. I ponder whether
I should order lumber and glass to be delivered——
or LEGO kits if necessary——to add a rumpus room
if this goes on much longer. Stocked with Twister
and Jenga, Risk and Sorry! Doubles as a Zen retreat.
Namaste. Let me out.

Liaisons Ordinaires

Apathy Breaks Up with Me

I'm no fun anymore, she says.
I care too much, which hobbles
or hastens the time we have together
and that's even more exhausting than acting
like it matters.   She says *Why*
> *are you so concerned with what might happen?*
> *Who do you think you are right now when you're with me*
> *that's any different than that time you were so bored*
> *you asked me out?*
>   *Sunsets?   Really?*
> *O and don't get me started with all your talk of souls*
> *and symphonies. How about just plowing into that line*
> *of pedestrians like web used to? What did it matter?*
> *They were chaff, their skins needed more tattoos. Where*
> *are you at, moonfed fool?*

>   The answer I'd give if I thought
>   she'd bother to listen goes something
>   like
>> *Y'know that empty silence we've sat in,*
>> *wallowed in, even called luxury? Turns out*
>> *I should've listened better and without you*
>> *because there was birdsong beneath the spirals*
>> *we spun, Ariels always available wherever*
>> *I could have asked for courage. Go on,*
>> *vamoose, Lowlife. Please.*

I Wish You Were You

when the whispers swirled about you and you could
not have cared any less than if they were raindrops disappearing
down the gutters of our local mall.

I wish bad men's monuments comprised of equal parts
tin and the Peter Principle could be melted down into
whistles, Slinkies, and medals for the least harm done.

I wish your words were View-Master reels——multidimensional,
stereoscopic, compassionate
as virtuous reality would allow, and all titled *Welcome*.

I wish TikTok was nitrate film and would vanish like
flash paper before the eyes of anyone who used them
to watch cyberbullies lip-synch a Kid Rock Republirant.

I wish we were us again instead of our shadows. I wish
you were the weather and here. I wish I was abundance.
I wish our whispers swirled over these sheets.

Lunacized

    After Andrew Wyeth's *Moon Madness*

Full moon through frosted window fills my eyes,
and midnight's whitecaps lift my body to behold
a surge of spilled light from the milk-silver surface
reflected in icicles hemming the old house.

So the moon is in this man again, wringing sense
from most senses as I'm struck into some loony pose
before a quivering mirror of oddball intentions,
agog at the shimmer on the stucco wall just outside.

The weight of tides synchronizes with a wait
for sugar plum fairies dancing on the keys
of a crystal celesta, and I accede to the albedo
of my fondest satellite, thrilled by its citron wax.

Come share such moony seduction with me
under what Emily called *her silver will*,
beneath this twinkling trove of winter's lamps,
delighted to be our own favorite lunatics.

So

So the blade of red flint
aglow with last night's questions
tempered by our fear's pitiful smoke
is sheathed.

We each stop, prepare
a plate of toast and a face
to tell one another
goodmorning.

We were midnight-loud,
indeed we were
whetting the edges
of some knife we could not bear
not to brandish like a prison shank
back and forth.

We are morning-subdued,
staring, diverting, mono-
and disyllabic enough to mutter
so. sorry.

Breathing Rooms

When it started, and we didn't know yet
what *It* would be, we continued as we
were used to——and except for setting up
an Instacart account, buying the wrong
masks in bulk, no longer hearing the rhyme
in *room* and *zoom*——we assumed our wonted
respective (respectful? respectable?)
positions: you upstairs on the desktop
behemoth, me downstairs on my raddled
recliner/lapdesk/laptop combo. We
hadn't yet learned what *doomscrolling* was. Oh
and yes, we still shared the meal prep, laundry
duty, thermostat patrol, choice of what
to watch on TV, same bed as always.

Then came disinfection of groceries,
self-mandated Zoom meetings, home-testing,
bread-baking, paring book-and-magazine
overflow, frightful FaceTiming to see
if she, he, they were okay anytime
cable news anchors announced new outbreaks.
And We. Just. Stopped meeting each other's eyes.
Inhabiting the same room if we could
avoid it. Touching so often. Sharing
stupid jokes and memories we'd built from
decades of Being Together, then off
to work, play rehearsals, watching people
be as absurd as we recognized in
our fool selves. As if Someone were flipping
B-movie calendar pages, only in slo-mo,
and the rooms had changed shape
from rectangles into rhomboids, and we lost
the thread of us. Then one late afternoon
without meaning to, we just didn't, and

one of us, out of muscle memory
or downright desire, reached the other's cheek,
then neck, then all the rest and so to bed.
The next morning arrived and we both went
to the megamarket before the crowds,
remembered to mask up, decided to
be done with sanitizing celery,
considered attending a poetry reading
or book club meeting in person
to admire the acoustics of the rooms.
This afternoon we will likely discuss
the themes of a play we went to last night——
loss, aging, confinement, doing with less,
the aftermath of a nuclear tide——
as well as our latest outrage at so
many dictators' cruelties, our next
attempt at air travel, what might bloom next
in the backyard. What may be unsaid, but
not unrealized: the breathing wonders
we have become together and counting.

Insectaria

We meet unawares, breathe to and fro like crickets.
Our appendages round the tones as we stroke music
from our wings, play with the light, play the earth
like the large drum it is, find the xylophones
under its skin, feel them resonate a final chord
before we rise and part.

Our lives are double circles interlacing
each morning. Midnight nectar's fervor draws us,
near-drowns us so that we can live under wonder,
warm ourselves while we fall asleep, eyes open
like birds borne in updrafts.

In all humility, we fly because we must
find each other anywhere there is air
and fluid fire in songs we recall
as we let them play us,
catch their refrains
like drifted breaths,
like gifts that rise from earth again
with wings we were unaware
we had all along.

Sonnet Catch XXII from the Papuese

after J. Heller and E. B. Browning

When our two spirits drift at last between
the grin of moon, chagrin of spring's full sun,
winking, shimmering, mousy hair undone,
our sainted Margaret Mead, free love's queen,
shall break into fire, bid us be obscene
but not heard in the flames we will have spun.
If angels' only ecstasy is one
doxology after another, lean
closer, my dark love——let us be well-damned
as we do our earthly joys consummate,
as we don't pretend we are not enjambed
in our contrarious conjoined checkmate,
eager to be islands undiagrammed,
sweating spirits gods dare not isolate.

When You I

Decades back you heard it in some psych class
maneuvered to curtail stress and assuage
your fellow students: the beige *I-Message*
that allowed the prof to feign real concern
disguised as Good Orderly Direction
and assertive non-aggression.

> *What I*
> *hear you saying,*

you'd say to Dr. G———,

> *is that conflicts*
> *like this one should be tabled*
> *until we all have time to consider*
> *a proper resolution*

and you'd think

> *This here's bushwah,*
> *Brother.*

So the Seventies became us
now in our past-seventies
as we try not to hurt one another
any more than we have already.

So I say,

> *When you decide in company*
> *what we will do next without turning to me, I*
> *feel invisible and/or absent.*

Such faces as we have these days are saved. Gears shift.
Passive voices wax into active listening,
alive as any sigh just about to suffocate
two candles set on a supper table.
We are well past the affective domain
by this time. When you ask for the safety
matches, I reach into my pocket.

When you say
   Strike
I suggest
   Anywhere.

Widow's Weeds

Drunk on tawny port,
face down in the canal,

only a foot deep and he drowned,
the bastard, and I loved him

and I guess I have to do that some more,
but I'm getting outta this valley,

go anywhere that doesn't require irrigation,
no place that knows about such awful wine——

the Israeli desert, maybe,
a high-rise with a rotating restaurant,

a town with a new agenda
full of men with some sense

and a healthy fear of water,
where I can wear basic black

and lavender.

You Are Right, Of Course

Otherwise, you'd still be talking to him,
and he'd still be listening. How often
has this happened——he, messing up,
you, clamping your lips till jaw muscles
bulge, words exploding later when others
aren't around to hear you be right again
at peak volume? Right now it's midnight,
and your anger and his contrition will
take their course, and of course all of both
will be authentic, then you each will rest right
through till the alarm clock startles you again,
and you start all over again till the next time
he messes up and you are right again perforce.

Your Fellow Traveler

I wake up with a start and remember
we were quarreling over our creeds.
The signs along this county road
tell us the miles we must go till
we can stretch and slacken our thin
skins. Meanwhile I am warm and cozy
enough on my side and your smile
tells me you don't mind driving a bit
further. Our destination is not yet
on any map we can unfold and say *There*.
Or at least that is what we believe
in this car built overseas sometime
during the second Clinton administration,
its steering still intact enough to shudder
through ruts and potholes the cattle trucks
have gouged into grooves we recall from
fifty-plus summers past. Ahead the road
wakens true as broken lines, wide enough
to rev up, climb and coast each small rise
as far as sunlight and high beams can carry us.

Try This

Stare at her without wanting more time.

Wake up anywhere not wondering
what she will do when she wakes.

Walk along a dirt road, shell beach, hallway
unaware of her flesh sliding to your skin,
joining, lingering at heart's center.

Stand near jasmine or rose,
breathe through to the air she lives in,
and do not dance to her pulse.

Write about any of this
and do it justice.

Valentines

By now we're well past launching, then scuttling
resolutions. Daffodils have erupted
a week before I take down the last
outside Christmas light strands,
unwinding 600 tiny bulbs
'round our Rose of Sharon tree,
trying not to tread on the yellow trumpets
that border its bulk and promise of amethyst bugles
in early summer. You are inside ready to begin
a quilt for our second granddaughter who'll arrive
amidst our atmosphere in mid-April.
Right now, though, you and I marvel
at this wrinkled grey ultrasound image
of her face, our first introduction to her,
she whose names we don't yet know.
We stand close. Simply holding the same
plain breath, we are easy with each other
 in this common moment built, as Mary Oliver said,
entirely out of attentiveness.
Now aware we need to, we finally exhale
the past. We find ourselves in each other's
shiny sloppy eyes. We find ourselves
likely to resolve we will remember
to do something about Valentine's Day.
Maybe we will. Maybe this instant is it,
and we have found all we need.

Ready to Step Into Waves

Brood

Take it easy, but take it
—— *Woodrow Wilson Guthrie*

We gather these breaths to us——
cup or corral our acuities in,
our sighings away from the kin
by whom we assume we are adopted,
to whom we have adapted.
Our nest is in our lungs, where is room enough
for each regard, each fancy to bring itself forth.

We are made kindred by the air we take,
brethren in fact because we brood and dwell
on each other's well-being. How long this takes
to inhere, to be a house that holds each adherent
secure and warm, then releases to a world so bone-cold
each breath can be seen, if only for a blink at the burning.

We are sisters too in truth, nursing each other
after that other first breath we draw.
If all we ever have is what we trade invisibly
in our hulls of flesh and fluidity, we can learn
to care for what we have. We can partake
our full portion as family. We can breathe easy.

Renascence

The rain had stopped, the mist swirled back to earth.
The sun hung stranded in the dead blue sky,
yet all that morning felt like a rebirth.

And those I passed seemed capable of mirth,
though they nor I could voice a reason why
the rain had stopped, the mist swirled back to earth.

The silence sought comrades and found a dearth
of quiet brothers midst the passersby,
yet all the morning felt like a rebirth.

We seek a family, a kindred's berth,
whatever truth we find inside each lie;
the rain had stopped, the mist swirled back to earth.

The globe is but a growth of each child's worth,
and each child fails, and some may die,
yet all that morning felt like a rebirth.

We all are strangers, cousins, common earth,
we speak each other's silences and sigh.
The rain has stopped, the mist swirls back to earth,
and all this morning feels like a rebirth.

Annus Mirabilis

after Dryden, after Whitman

how can these
not be miracles———

————the chance to drive an unknown
neighbor to the nearest hospital

————that tiny string of tomato seeds
you planted in early April then tended as they punched
their way up   out   into the shape of grapes
with their taste of red pearls
served gratefully in patio shade
as sacramental caprese

————those well-deep voices
those doleful eyes that hold multitudes of ancestors
beaten   lynched   bothered to death or life inside
a concrete coop   who still find the unadorned grace
and strength to rise up   out   into our souls
make them open   march   work for a justice
delayed   denied   all with one song   one long
full breath at last

————the spark inside
citizens' bitter sighs of clarity
as elected pettifoggers acquit
a cruel regime's *quid pro quo*

————the luck to heed three stutter-trills
of a single goldfinch   then that abrupt blizzard
of small birds   all the bright and quiet small things
we make time for now

    ——a shuddering brush against
other supermarket humans as we
all of us push our poor wonky carts
bend to choose a likely orange
smile behind our masks hoping
it is heard as we all wait in line

    ——those same folks' stamina sufficient
to register both evil and that still small voice without despair
or apathy on behalf of what is worthy and may last

    ——an omnidirectional Zoom birthday party of a
granddaughter with 25 relatives from all over
singing the longest song in the world out of sync
out of tune and laughing tearing up as the girl shrieks
at the candle on her smash cake

    that moment we wake to find
    that moment we move toward
    that moment we write down
      embrace
      shake off
      grasp
      it's not too late
      to find a next
      moment

  and the year not half gone

Seated by a Window in Southwest Seattle

The mountains are out, they say here on these mornings
the sun deigns to make distance visible.
The snowpack sketchbook of the Cascade Range reveals
the peaks now, and more things seem possible.

Crows, then ravens stir the firmament.
Red cedar treetops blink and twitch,
stretch themselves all the way down
so gruffly even the sorrel at their base shivers.

I suppose I should be out and about
my own mountain of métier,
so I position my clumsy pinions,
flap, blunder, twinge a bit,
heft my lumbering way at a horizon
I can just now make out.

Intravenous

The anesthetic does its work
as I wait for the surgeon.
I can touch the ocean now,
walk right into the next wave
up to my chest and feel
my salt meld into its salt,
accept myself as crystalline,
vital, a vessel carrying, being
carried by a sea's urges
to reach and be reached,
steered by the moon's water
pulsing, clear, on.

Letting Go Gladly

Fare thee well, moose-sized mug from Vermont,
you two jumbo flagons with embossed elephants,
you recognition-of-service quartet of cups with
15/20/25/30-Years emblazoned, reminding us
each morning how much coffee was required
to survive five years on the same job *ad absurdum*,
as well as you lot, you round-bottomed pots
and skillets warped by being plunged too soon
into sick-and-tired sink water.

You all served your purposes passably, and we
are beholden to every scald and crack you suffered
on our behalf, each stain you sustained that we never
scrubbed enough to honor your worth. *Enfin*,
please know we loved to hold you, use you, see you
where we sometimes remembered you belonged.
Please accept our praise, such as it is. We are not
mindful enough to have deserved you, so beg
your pardon as we box you up to leave on the curbside.

We console ourselves by supposing nothing and no one
is irreplaceable. In due time our cracks and crinkles
will undo us, and we will be left in some container,
drained of whatever we held that was useful here,
still glad we were here long enough.

This Afternoon

The pasture has erupted in what my father called
poor man's cotton——a joke he whispered every time
we saw a field of dandelions nod and drift away
parachute by parachute.

There are too many to launch the way I used to:
target a steady tunnel of breath at a fragile globe of fluff
till everything in front of me expands to migrating seeds,
contracts to remnant stalk.

Crows cling to sky or familiar branches as their shadows
settle their black steel voices into clicking colloquy. Beaks
like batons conjure strange needs into auguries of incidents
somber, ulterior.

Midafternoon, and all that presages sundown——smaller
birds scuttling under live oaks, ripe peaches succumbing
to autumn and gravity, a *clack* of almonds hitting the tarps
or the unlucky hatless farmer.

Beyond this tableau, these puffweeds whisper their nicknames
to the still-drifting florets spilling themselves completely until
their onboard hope born of a sharp williwaw descends,
declares Spring.

Hugely Beautiful

> *Although it is only a little planet,*
> *it is hugely beautiful.*
>   —*Lawrence Collins*

Such a scintilla, this bluebell by the side of the trail
ringing in the morning with its clustered cousins
beside the jack pines that point to the rumpled summits.

Then a frisson of what you take for déjà vu
slips into your bones at the sight of a pika
as he scoots across a morning glacier, then pauses.

Between the slow smithereens of stony loam
and the rough-legged hawk's nest made of sticks
and bones drift the motes of our skin and smoke.

Specks of first sunlight, flecks of gloaming shadow
enter the infinitesimal instances we are given
to learn a trace more of this precious fair earth.

My Best Impersonation of a Harbor Seal

Basking belly up on this soft beach
of an Adirondack chaise,
chewing sturdy cold brew coffee
from a glass meant for parfait,
I use my front flippers
to wave away noisome flies
or turn pages of poems about seafood,
the breeze just cool, just warm enough,
the sunlight oblique enough that I sigh,
feel completely unendangered,
unaware of the word *calendar*.
The thing called *tomorrow* will nudge me
soon enough, make me haul myself out
pinnipedally, make my blubbery lurch
belly down, nose and whiskers protruding,
focusing on an unholidayed future,
reluctantly growing fingers again.

Rationalism

after Jane Kenyon

If bats were peonies,
we would plant them year after year,
gather them into batquets
which would also warn us of danger
with their organic sonar.

When the full moon stares us down,
we will behold which ones
have turned their heads to smile darkly,
evaded our reach to reap them,
letting us be near, not with them.

They are here to remind us
how many mysteries we need
to sustain us, why subjunctive tenses were
invented, where present fragrances ascend
on future wings as we go back to work.

The Nut Grass Groove

I'm inclined to agree with Miss Maudie——
    Why, one sprig of nut grass can ruin a whole yard.
The world's worst weed, and
I'm pulling it from all the spots in my yard
where it meets soil. I'm also
troweling it up from ten inches down,
where those sly black nuts launch
their tentacled tendrils to prove to me
God's inescapable sense of humor:
no matter the human assiduity,
leverage, herbicide, or hope,
nut grass negates human effort.
I think——*Prayer is for larger matters, but*
    Lord, show me the way.
And I guess the Lord does,
but not in the way I prayed.
Now I am in the nut grass groove,
that personal human rhythm
that finds them in their secret slender
peek-a-boo whatcha-gonna-do
arsenals, and removes them cleanly
to the eye alone, admitting at last
to myself they will be back,
simultaneously acknowledging
to them with a smirk,
so will I.

Epistolary

The scratches on the cracked pane the birds keep thudding against are mine. That time before the first month of COVID confinement ended, when the pane was clean and the world sure wasn't. Call it cabin fever as the urge to let the world know I could still scrawl and scratch some sense out of fear's whirligig gripped my hand, said *Let the birds know, at least.* At first it was breath-fog, my finger squeaking out the *HE* of *HELP*, then dithering it into *HERE* and finally into *HOPE* as I wondered *HOPE what?*

Then I wised up a bit, realized the birds would have to read it backwards and *HOPE* would fade. I opted for something more permanent, first a scarlet Sharpie and a slow widdershins memo to goldfinches, scrub jays, Anna's hummingbirds——*Hope your skies are azure and your feeders full.* The finches will have to translate for the mourning doves, who are too hard of thinking to comprehend. Since even Permachrome is eventually soluble, the letters ran down the pane like a hemorrhage of whispers. After fine-tip ballpoints and gel pens failed, I last-resorted to scratching out a pushpin screed no longer directed to the birds, but to firmament and silver-greyed cirruses, whatever expanses might care that I was below and breathing, writing *The scratches on the cracked pane the birds keep thudding against are mine.*

This morning four days before official autumn, first raindrops tell their truths slant, type their own text against this sheet of what was one man's half-mirror. Jasmine and nutgrass, redbud leaves and the last of the rosebuds stir and shine. What will be the winter garden——once I pry yellowed tomato plants and their cages from sun-cracked soil——readies itself for snow peas, Swiss chard, something new I've never planted, all the shoots that will surprise come that as-yet-unwritten morning when new green hope scratches its way skyward, scrawls *here*. Till then, we'll wash our hands, faces, clothes, windows when we can, walk outside like autumn's liturgists while the petrichor is fresh and we are too.

In Which I Imagine Writing at a Standing Desk

cobbled from the bifold closet door that needs painting
most, unsprung from its hinges and placed on the fifth
rungs fashioned from wooden peach ladders set just so,
typing on my 42-pound 1917 Underwood Herniator
bought for 50 bucks, praying its actions and my own
synch for once.

My adlibbed escritoire bows in the middle from the metal beast's
heft as I pummel out a couple stanzas built of yesterday's inertia till
the entire assemblage becomes
a trampoline of 30-pound paper, brimful coffee mug,
Eberhard Faber eraser, and pocket thesaurus.

I wait for the third stanza to settle itself and glance at
a cardinal as it bobs on a pink dogwood branch outside
the window well-used for early morning jumpstart stabs
at something sensible to say about the transitory nature
of flight or life or absurdly colorful birds.

The fourth stanza starts with images of Muppet balloons chasing
and replacing the ladders, the typewriter's innards
now transparent as vials of new ice, everything afloat and
alight with alternatives to the familiar lap desk, laptop,
lack of luster or legerdemain, alive with the ready wonder
of what may happen next.

Mense Octobri Gratiae

On this teetering autumn morning I am beholden
        to contraries——

house wren in a bubble-scat duet with mockingbird
        atop enameled tomato cages
blood-soaked feathers lying jig-sawed under the feeder
        as grey tuxedo cat licks her clotted muzzle
Rose of Sharon hovers its chiffon above
        the cracked driveway
again the gangrenous oil spews into our fretful sea
        and we act astounded or blasé
General Sherman Sequoia adjusts his aluminum skirt
        in strict time ready for the fire dance
murky autumn sky bristles to choke us
        with outstretched talons
two years' worth of wonder as she blows bubbles, asks
        Why ah bubbles?
smarmy din and shriek of *right-to-life* as
        our children starve invisibly
roly poly hours enough to mosey to
        a fresh museum of redemption
shiny promises hang like crow tinsel
        from the senator's pre-election maw
blue air all day long
        aroma of sewage and Subway bread
this photo of us in Edinburgh
        pleased with ourselves——
                you in your soft-as-ciselé beret
                me in my herringbone Kirk cap
Josh Ritter singing
        Joy to the city
        the parking lot lights
        the lion of evening with the rain in its eyes
        Joy to the freeway and joy to the cars
        Joy to you baby wherever you are tonight tonight tonight

squadron of mosquitoes
        in love with you tonight
any valley oak leaf as it lets go,
        tumbles toward the earth that birthed it
all nutgrass and nettles as they jab skyward
        any winter garden seed as it shivers toward sun
all death cap mushrooms lurking biliously
        under live oak

In today's steady silent dusk I am beholden to beauty
        that breathes any way it can——
In death's belly carrion beetles colonize
        in all their iridescence
Young couples in their tattooed twenties
        glisten as they dance
Grasses devour broken bottled alleys
        turn them into spring
Needles   masks   Lysol   scarlet-black skirts
        with six-foot radii

The word *raze* as in
        emaciated housing projects *in extremis*
the word *raise* as in
        winter gardens of beets/spinach/carrots/squash
            for those who can't

Upper Falls, Lower Falls, Valley Floor

Water comets over the edge,
and we below cannot believe
it does not burst
into flaming petals of ice——
true aquatechnics old as magma
underneath, forming forever
what is seen now——
flow and fall and wonder
simple, grand, alive,
and since it lives, must weep
for its very completion.

Low Arcanum

> *I've got a secret, I shouldn't tell,*
> *I'm gonna go to heaven in a split-pea shell.*
> *——Elizabeth Cotten, Fred Neil*

Forget faith as mustard seed. A pawned watch
with its innards abuzz on a dull shelf
can tell a time to remove doubt's mountains.
Riddle what else can be saved by two hands.

Transparency reveals what, exactly?
Paltry blisters in windows and lenses?
What to do after the puzzle's pieces
jig into an unsilvering mirror?

After all that sugaree we've shaken,
the shame we shuffle in place of dancing
as we ought now, there's still an elixir——

go on, sing some mysteries till they're yours
to let go. Then keep humming so they've gone
on to be someone else's tune and fuel.

Some Prayers on a Monday

She bows her head to watch
beet seedlings jitter in the breeze.

                He closes his eyes,
counts twenty seconds to retain some ghost of
Because I could not stop for Death, opens them, looks
at the sky——still there.

            They light a candle when the grid
goes down.

              You wince when the wheelchair rides wonky,
smile when you see green just ahead.

                  I doubt doubt doubt
this gloaming is worth its stars, await await still await
what I might call a full breath.

              We vibrate to the buzz of
flying jewels keen for nectar.

              She kneels to the work at hand,
all shoulders and full arms, thinks of thanks as deep suds.

                      He steers stiffly
down the middle lane of 99 through the dust devils, then loosens
his death-grip clench on the wheel
to see better.

            They puff steam from the corn chowder,
sprinkle bacon or basil as elements of the Eucharist
they need to face the long night together.

                                              You hear
breezes free of quarantine or flexion of gloved fingers
and hum till the key changes.

                                                  I twilight-sleep through
adjustment and release, and my muscles know me
as I rouse and rise.

                                  We don't know enough,
                                  so we pray we might live by
                                  all we offer next.

Towards the Splendid City
(Nobel Lecture, December 13, 1971)

I do not know whether I experienced this or created it,
I do not know whether it was truth or poetry,
something passing or permanent,
the poems I experienced in this hour,
the experiences which I later put into verse.
  ——*Pablo Neruda*

Santiago. Stockholm.
Antipodean, yes, and arduous,
and yet *Yes* to the distance,
the landscape and solitude
in those neighborhoods of words,
and *Yes* to the dawns where Rimbaud
beheld his own *ville splendide*
with such *ardente patience*——
that burning patience vital
to receive all vision and carry it on.

And I have fidgeted my face to squint out something
of the bright metropolis these poets pictured,
gone wild-eyed and slack-jawed whenever I fancied
I could tend such a flame alive inside, the one I saw
rising from their fierce words, or inside cataracts
and cardinals, then stalled, doubted my soul, hand, breath
could shape a vessel that would carry light, might serve
in a struggle to build more. Too seldom, I have reached out
to hope's edges or listened deep and long for love to appear,
only to remember suddenly the light was all around,
the strange music was waiting to be joined.

And so *yes* to Pablo's *blue heaven above,*
a generous stream of light unimpeded
by leaves, reaching even to the mystery
of an ox's eye sockets, to campfire guitars'
smoldering songs, and to cave embers
that join together to keep darkness cornered,
to rickety spans where we dare
our clumsy dances——all so we can see
these common enchantments as
our *most ancient rites of conscience,*
so we may share them, so we may
continue our journey ablaze with
well-lit words, lives of plain splendor.

The Eyebrows On It

> *Writing about music is like dancing about architecture.*
> *——Martin Mull (sometimes attributed to Frank Zappa)*

Nevertheless, there are notes and verbs that have
cohabited. "You Really Got Me" tells us
everything we need to know about lust
and power chords, how distortion can
clarify, and even *I* can dance to it.

    Other verses, other choruses, Greek or
    gospel, conclude only when all the truth's
    been called out, responded to
    as its echoes ripple, remind us
    Chorus once hinted both song and dance.

And lyrics? Ginsberg's *first thought, best thought*
turns out not to work all that well all the times
we think our rough draft or featured solo is good
enough. One line does not a libretto make.
Remember Aristotle's swans and summers.

    We need bright songs, best words, grand voices,
    but not only. Zappa called this The Attitude.
    His musicians' catchphrase: *putting the eyebrows*
    on it——that synchrony of everyone's promise
    achieved in exquisite performance.

Who will sing our stanzas, write our refrains when
pop is past and rap is on all required reading lists?
Which tunes will need eyebrows? What machines
will fabricate them? Meanwhile, drop pen,
lose baton. Just listen. Grass is tuning up.

Uncertainty

To be as I was taught or know I ought——ah, that is the
inquest I enter whenever I can't find a rulebook. I am on vacation,
I am told, and should have packed all I thought
I would need, but something Other told me I should leave room
for surprise. If I know where I'm going and what
I'll require once I'm there, why go?

Maybe my doubtfulness stems from another need——
to be safe and sure while reckoning I risk a new discovery. This La
Jolla afternoon I descend three tiers of crumbling concrete steps
onto a beach new to me. The steps are
stippled with Mason sand like sugar grains, treacherous
enough that I could misstep and fall shamefully. At the bottom is
an unsullied strand made of even finer grains,
deep and deceptive enough to wrench my ankle if I don't tumble
headlong anyway.

I imagine arriving at tideline in time to see the green flash at
sunset——that brief phenomenon of horizon light at the frontier
between sun and moon. I tell myself I might just be *transformed*,
and *ascertain* myself as to whether I am punctual,
so I accelerate. I am early, apparently. I have not stumbled,
wrung any muscles, am no more imbalanced than when I was
overwary, but have not attained enlightenment, haven't felt
any *Aha!*s, am no more mindful. I am only alone and standing at
a seashore breathing, watching waves on a planet generally more
certain of its purpose than I, and just as mortal. If this
is what I ought to be without being told, it is enough for now.

> Sunset assurance——
> simply respiring, ready
> to step into waves.

Zehn Gebehtsachen (Ten Prayer Things)

Prayer Bicycle

Two wheels round, rounder,
rounding toward a home
of questions making answers
on two wheels filled with prayer.

Prayer Pillow

Rest your head and hands here.
Bow as low as needed——no more.
Stay awake long enough. Finish
one prayer before you open another.
Recollect your fellow children, how
some of them exited too soon, too poor,
how you might have helped them
with more alms. This is why
we all have need of rest.

Prayer Woodstove

Start with small matters,
like beholding motes
adrift atop tinder
you place as a base
of what will catch and blaze.
Remember to breathe in accord
with stouter branches you stack next.
Weightier chunks of wood and words
are last, to sustain your conversation
with all sacred things. Watch smoke rise.
See what you have done, are doing,
is part of it all.

Prayer Turret

No ivory castle, no
isolation booth, no escape disguised
as sanctuary, this place could be
underground and still serve as a turret.
It is meant to hold certain plain tools
and you as you use them.
Begin with the plainest, the sharp one——
which could be called *humility*
if it weren't so busy being itself.

Prayer Cacti

These will flower, yes,
but as slowly
as they sport thorns.
We defend ourselves,
we say our thorns
are natural to us,
yet we expect
to be embraced
for our redolence
of clear grace.
Therefore, pray piecemeal,
with fewer points.

Prayer Stetson

Make sure it fits
the occasion, much more
than its display as headpiece alone.
When it gets dusty and sweaty, as it should,
be sure that is due to much use outside.

Prayer Rocking Chair

Sometimes it will creak, travel every so often
unexpectedly. The rockers might wear
unevenly. This is all right.
It was never meant to be
a stationary glider.
Find your rhythm,
feel the prayer
lulling you inside again, again.

Prayer Candle

This is simple. Check the wick
for length. Find your flint and iron.
Strike anywhere. Rouse the flame.
Let it light the corners.

Prayer Bucket

This is for reaching into,
pulling forth what is needed
to make sense of emptiness elsewhere.
It need not be full, only filling
and put to good use. Kneel
when feasible. Mind the joys
you carry in such a plain pail.
They will keep the sorrows company.

A Respiration

O
Yes
we breathe
in a circle
built of just before loss
and what becomes of us
as some light
pries steadily into
our long stubborn clutch
on our grief like a diploma
till we can undo our dark surety
let go of dear death
risk a soul as yet unsteady
unfamiliar
unshaped
unloved
Soon enough
though not as we
would have it
gratitude exhales its *anima*
and we heal
or at least inhale daybreak
built of just common grace
circling and settling
like prayer——
O
Yes

Epilogue: Widdershins

I cleave time to read some poetry not my own
as ripe lemons droop and thrash in the rain
from their spiky branches thin as green twine.
The pewter-and-white cat who wishes to live here
peers in through the sliding glass door, almost
trustful. Puckered recycling bins lean askew
in the street, awaiting the next serrated gust
to right them. Windchimes peal for some chance
to celebrate while other musics make themselves
from velocity and open tuning. Motley-colored
mini-lights hammer-strung to our house's stucco
hold their own against today's downpour. Black
cotton masks fester in each downstairs room,
plus three in each sedan——not enough. Today
courage looks like breathing through any layers
compassion and anticipation can't crack. I wrote
this poem backwards and forwards like a prayer
to poetry not my own.

Gratitudes

    Now and always, I am breath-to-breath grateful to Susan for loving me and letting me be her husband all these years, and to Graham, Mark, Dina, Orly, and Penny for their love, support, and tolerance for having a poet as a relative.

    Sincere thanks to Monika Rose and Manzanita Writers Press for your acceptance of this book and for your sage editorial guidance toward its publication.

    Deep appreciation to my dear friend and fellow poet Linda Toren for your skill as a writer, your grace toward my poetry, and your dedicated encouragement concerning this collection.

    Special thanks to Jack Sutton for his sharp photographic sensibilities and Ann Williams-Bailey for her marvelous cover art.

    Manifold gratitudes to Lee Herrick, Kai Coggin, and Tama L. Brisbane for your friendship in taking time to read these poems and for writing your gracious comments.

    I am forever beholden to fellow poets, theater friends, and other artists for their wisdoms, inspirations, bright flames, and best human hearts. You have inspired, guided, and kindly supported my own voice as a writer——whether you knew it or not. Thank You, Modesto-Stanislaus Poetry Center poets, my fellow Licensed Fools, the All Our Words poetry critique group, Prospect Theater Project, Merced Shakespearefest, Carnegie Arts Center, Left Margin Lit, Tupelo Press' 30/30 Project, The Writing Salon, 24PearlStreet, Home Grown . . .

    I am thankful for the new young poets, playwrights, actors, musicians, painters, photographers, and other artists who are creating wonder-filled work now and for the future, and who will, as Gil Turner's old folk ballad asserted, *carry it on* . . .

    Thanks, finally, as always, to you reading this book; I am much obliged——and still rejoicing.

Acknowledgements

I am very grateful to these literary journals and their editors for publishing these poems, some in earlier forms:

"A Casino in Gomorrah"
Atticus Review

"I Wish You Were You"
Mockingheart Review

"Sonnet XXII from the Papuese"
More Than Soil, More Than Sky: The Modesto Poets

"In Which I Imagine Writing at a Standing Desk"
Verse-Virtual

"Gullywasher"
River Heron Review

"This Afternoon" and "Renascence"
Monterey Poetry Review

"Widow's Weeds"
Barzakh Magazine

"Seated at a Window in Southwest Seattle"
Blue Heron Review

"A Respiration"
The Banyan Review

About the Author

Gary Thomas grew up on a peach farm outside Empire, California. Prior to retirement, he taught eighth grade language arts for thirty-one years and junior college English for seven. He has presented poetry workshops for literary organizations, festivals, and conferences. His poems have been published or accepted for publication in *The Comstock Review, MockingHeart Review, Atticus Review, River Heron Review, Barzakh, Blue Heron Review, Split Rock Review, Book of Matches, Hole in the Head Review*, and *The Banyan Review* among others, and in the anthology *More Than Soil, More Than Sky: The Modesto Poets*. He is a founding member of the Modesto-Stanislaus Poetry Center (MoSt) and of the Stanislaus County writing group known as The Licensed Fools. A full-length collection, *All the Connecting Lights*, was released in August 2022 from Finishing Line Press.

www.ingramcontent.com/pod-product-compliance
Lightning Source LLC
Chambersburg PA
CBHW061803070526
44586CB00023B/2691